# Freedom between -

## Baseball and the Native American Boarding School Experience

Written by Gregory Rubano
Illustrations by Jerry Aissis

Copyright © 2014 by Dr Gregory Rubano
All rights reserved.

ISBN-13: 978-1500530563
ISBN-10: 1500530565

MW01118061

I round third base.
Your throw speeds toward my heart.
My spikes shower the earth with itself.
My keen eyes are on the target.

Home I stand.
Free.

How to beat me?
Run faster.
Throw the ball harder.
Hit the swiftly moving circle more squarely.

As he got off the village-on-wheels, he felt their eyes looking at him.

Some whispered.

Some pointed.

None smiled.

He was different, and it was clear in their eyes that different was not good.

3

When he touched the cold of the iron gates of the school's entrance, he knew he was far away from the gentle voices and hands of the loved ones that had guided him.

Would he ever again hear the laughter of his friends?

Would he ever again see the sparkling pride in his father's eyes?

In his starched collar, the Director of the School seemed very proud of who he was. "Boys and girls, you have traveled many miles for the privilege of attending this school. Here you will learn our language, our religion, and our ways of making a living. Now line up. Your clothes, your keepsakes, and all your belongings will be collected."

Staring down at them, the Director added, "Hide nothing."

The next morning, in front of everyone, they cut his long black hair. He heard snickering. He did not cry. Some did. He was handed a dull gray uniform. The girls were given dark dresses whose collars looked very stiff and very uncomfortable. Everyone looked alike. They marched to the cafeteria.

Talking was forbidden.

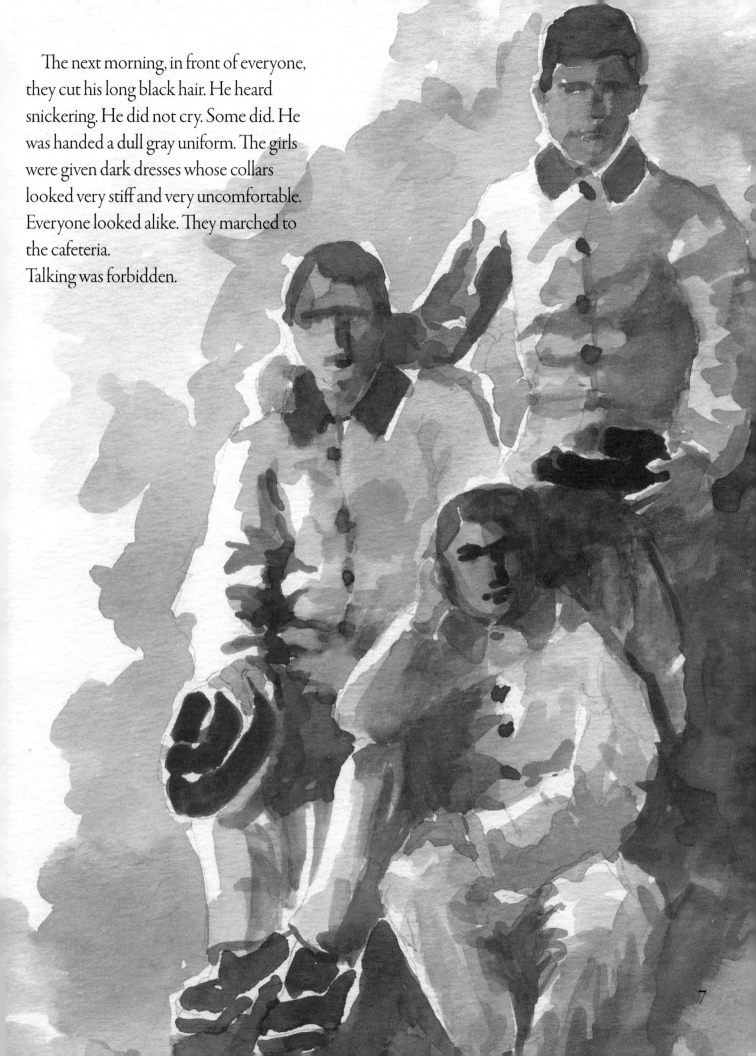

That afternoon, the Director looked down upon the boys and girls gathered in front of the bandstand. He seemed even taller than he did yesterday. "Much better, children. We are making progress." He leaned forward. "Now, there are a few rules at this school that you will not break. You will not dance the dances nor sing the songs you have been taught. You will not associate with members of your own tribe. You will not tell the meaningless stories you have been told by your parents and others. Most importantly, you will not speak your native language. Not in class. Not in your rooms. Not on the playing fields."

The Director held up a black book with many names listed in it. "When summer comes, you will be placed with families in the area. They will teach you how to be productive citizens learning a worthwhile trade."

He paused. "Understand that I am your school father. I know what is good for you."

The Director pointed across the lawn to a long one-story building across the green. "Defy me, and your home will be the guard house. It is not a pleasant place."

That afternoon one of the boys was sent to the guard house. Another was forced to stand for hours on his tiptoes with arms outstretched. Raising their eyes to look at him, his classmates nodded quickly as they passed by him like a silent stream.

That night, the moonlight bathed his room. It carried the sweet scented stories of his people. Stories of how the world began. Stories of great quests by proud warriors. Stories about the Great Spirit who lived inside the dark tasseled mane of the great elkhound, and who lived within his heart as well. He remembered with pride how his father's canoe was always the first into the blue quiet morning and the white moon sky.

Fearing the Director might hear his thoughts, he tightened his lips. Hard footsteps walked the halls and disappeared. When they did, he took from his pocket the stones he had removed from the necklace given to him by his mother. The stones were warm. He knew from what stream they had come. He and his brother had often fished in it. He listened to the soothing voices of the spirits that traveled in the singing water. He could also hear the sound of his father's and mother's laughter.

He smiled. Outsmarting the Director felt good.

Everything they owned had been thrown in one pile. The children strained to see what had been a part of them. The leather moccasins that carried the spirit of the thundering buffalo. The velvet sash woven by fingers that darted in and out like the snake among the whispering reeds. The proud hawk carved by a hand with deep rivers running through it.

The red of the fox. The blue of the sky. The green of the early corn. The brown of the bear. All of these and many other colors were a tapestry of memories that covered the earth before them.

The match lit the corner of a blanket. Traveling like the glittering gills of the fish between sun splashed river rocks, the light soon became a blazing consuming fire. The soft voices of their elders telling tales of mysterious people and beautiful things crackled as the smoke carried them to the darkening sky that would return them in the morning light.

The voice of the Man-in-the Stand once
again surrounded them. The colorless
pools of cold that were his eyes cracked.
"All that is Indian in you must die. We are
going to civilize you." Although he did not
know what the word "civilize " meant, each
child felt as if he were a bright cloth being
held under the muddy water until all its
color was gone. In similar boarding schools
across America, over 125,000 Native
American children felt the same.

Like a spider moving towards the struggling bug caught in its carefully spun web,

SHAME moved towards each one of them.

Standing on the warming brown earth and the spring grass, the boys made a line between the two square plates. Some were Chippewa. Some were Sioux. Some Pawnee. Some Apache. Some Wabanaki. Each was careful not to stand next to someone from his own tribe.

A voice spoke. "The games you have been taught are no more. They are games of backward people. Today, you will learn America's game- baseball. Play hard, and it will teach you the virtues of self-reliance, clean competition, and cooperation. It will teach you all that you are lacking."

Each boy was handed yet another uniform. This one was different though. The collars were soft, and the "C" seemed to curl like a startled snake ready to defend itself.

Their hits and throws streaked across the dusty sky. Each of them played hard. As they ran swiftly across the outfield with legs made strong from chasing the prey, as they struck the ball with wrists and arms made strong from pulling the bow, as they caught the ball darting at their feet like a rabbit running for cover, each began to feel the pulse of a warrior eager to prove himself. Quietly, just beyond the hearing of those sitting near, they spoke to one another words of challenge, of encouragement, of friendship. A few spoke in their native language.

One young man from the Chippewa tribe played especially well. Given the name "Mandalesce," or "little animal spirit," Charles Albert Bender was soon to show the world how good he was at "America's Game."

Because the Carlisle Indian School baseball team played stiff competition, including the best collegiate teams in the area, many soon knew that Charles could pitch like few others. Soon after leaving Carlisle, at the age of nineteen, he was asked to pitch for the Philadelphia Athletics of the American League. The manager of the team, Connie Mack, knew that for Charles to be successful he would need more than talent. He would have to have faith in himself when players and fans ridiculed his Native American heritage.

"Hey Injun, you're going to get scalped today!"

"Back to the wigwam with you and your squaw, Chief!"

Charles didn't say a word back. His face didn't show his anger and his heart didn't show its sadness. He stepped down from the mound. The stinging words hurt.

"Back to the reservation, Red Man!"

"Hey, Chief, wanna smoke a peace pipe?"

Mandalesce stepped back up onto the mound. He slammed the ball into his glove. The speed of his pitch pounded the catcher's leather mitt. "Strike three," yelled the umpire. The stadium was suddenly quiet.

Charles Albert Bender

Famous Chippewa
Won over

First pitcher in
of 6 games
to pitch 3
complete games....

Indian......
200 games...
World Series

Highest A.L. Percentages
in
1910-1911-1914......

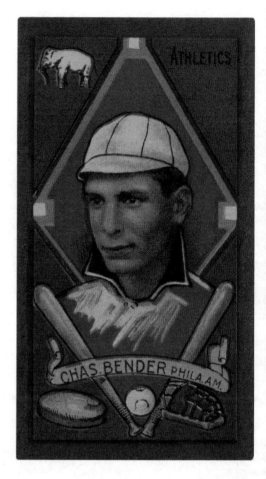

ATHLETICS

CHAS. BENDER PHILA. A.M.

Before his career was over, Charles Bender had won over 200 games, complied a 2.46 ERA, and led the American League in winning percentage in three different seasons. He invented a new pitch, the nickel curve, that is still being used today. The great Ty Cobb called him the most intelligent pitcher he ever faced. Charles was especially good in the high pressured environment of baseball's showcase- the World Series. He won six World Series games, averaging an ERA of 2.44, and completed 9 of the 10 games he pitched. In the 1905 World Series against the New York Giants, he pitched a 4 hit complete game shutout , and again went the distance in his second appearance, allowing only two runs . His ERA for the series was an astonishing 1.06!

After retirement, Charles Albert Bender was chosen to be a members of a special place that honored the very best in the game- the Baseball Hall of Fame. To fellow Hall of Famer Connie Mack, Charles Bender was the best money pitcher of them all, the one pitcher he wanted to be on the mound when the game was on the line. More importantly, Mr. Mack considered him the finest gentleman he had ever known. Charles' longtime roommate, Rube Bressler, agreed calling him "one of the finest and kindest men who ever lived."

A Penobscot Indian, Louis Sockalexis played three seasons for the Cleveland Spiders, posting a .338 batting average in 1897. Hall of Fame manager John McGraw said of him: "If Sock had stayed up for five years, he could have well been better than Cobb Wagner, or Babe Ruth."

"Bright Path" James Thorpe was born to Mary James, a Potawatomi Indian and descendant of the last great Sauk and Fox chief Black Hawk, a noted warrior and athlete. Thorpe played twenty seasons of minor and major league ball, starting with the New York Giants. After winning the Decathlon and the Pentathlon in the 1912 Stockholm Olympics, Jim was told by King Gustav V: "You, sir, are the greatest athlete in the world. I would consider it an honor to shake your hand."

A Cahuilla Indian from California, John Tortes Meyers played nine seasons in the big leagues, from 1909-1917. Educated at Darmouth, he was an important ingredient in the New York Giants championships seasons and was the catcher for the great Christy Mathewson. He compiled a .291 career batting average.

Playing ball for one season for the Philadelphia Athletics, Elijah Edward Pinnace was the first "full blooded" American Indian in the major leagues. Born in Walpole Island , Ontario, he played only two games but posted a 2.57 earned run average.

Although Albert Charles Bender is the only one in the Hall of Fame, over 120 Native Americans played professional baseball, including six from Carlisle. Countless others played on the many other teams spread across the country. As it did for Afro-American athletes who were to follow, baseball gave Native Americans a chance to compete fairly and fiercely. If society treated so many of them unjustly, at least on these ball fields, between these lines, nothing could be taken away from them.

A member of the Pawnee tribe, Mose Yellow Horse compiled an 8-4 record while pitching two seasons for the Pittsburgh Pirates in the 1920's. During that tenure, he struck out the mighty Babe Ruth,. The glove that Mose wore is now in the Baseball Hall of Fame, not too far from an exhibit that highlights the achievements of Charles Albert Bender.

The Way Mose Yellow Horse Learned how to Throw
Along Black Bear Creek in Pawnee, Oklahoma Before
He discovered the Meaning of a Fastball or Whistling
 - after Albin Leading Fox, Pawnee elder and relative of Mose Yellow Horse

Some mornings
There's a hint of myth in the air
The way
Horizons become
shapely pines,
The way
Blowing maple limbs
Turn their curved leaves
Into faces, like
Into exact profiles of crows
In flight. And farmyards
Are the cartography
Of childhood
In Indian Territory
A boy
Who is eight years old
Will quietly cross
Hid dad's (allotted) land with his hands full
Of round stones: he
Has heard enough stories
To imagine himself a hunter,
Enough of the old
That's the-way-it-went
To know how to track
A rabbit, squirrel, or snake.

And he
moves slowly
through the woods
with some kind of warrior
images twirling around his mind.
He will
return home
with an evening meal
of two rabbits & and crow
and tell his parents just how
he did I:
That bird
was a hundred feet away
sitting on a fence post,
and his parents will say
Good,
Now wash the dishes.
And he
learns how to whistle
from listening to rocks
fly out of his hand.

I have found my son
Playing ball with the rainbow belted Wabanaki.
The beautiful colors that spread over the sable field
Delight my eyes.
And in the middle of the night,
In the banquet room of the sparkling sky,

He stands.

Chief Morning Star
Chief of the Cheyenne people

# The Rest of the Story

## The Search for Solutions

In the mid-to-late nineteenth century, it was called "the Indian Problem." What was the government to do with the hundreds of thousands of Native Americans spread across the country, even as determined swarms of settlers marched in all directions? Living on ancestral land, with foreign customs, values and appearances that suggested just how uncivilized they were, Indians were a threat to the country's expansion and its destiny.

A solution had to be found.

No matter what the "solution" hatched by the government, Native Americans were to pay dearly.

## Before the Boarding Schools

Most governmental efforts to solve the Indian problem involved systematic efforts to eliminate the identity of the Native American populations. As early as the 1650's, "praying towns" were established in which Native Americans were removed from what was seen as the contamination of their own culture. In these towns, Native Americans were to be converted to civilized and godly people. There were fourteen such towns established in the colonies, most in Massachusetts.

Fully aware that the treatment of the Native Americans violated the human rights premises upon which the fledgling nation was ideologically based, President Washington took action. Recognizing them as leaders of sovereign nations, Washington negotiated a proposal with leaders of the Iroquois nation and other affected tribes, such as the Creeks and Cherokee. It called for the creation of two separate districts north and south of the Ohio River for the Native American population living east of the Mississippi. That populations numbered between 75.000 and 100, 000. The created territories would be out of bounds for the exploding populations of homesteaders pushing westward. The proposal fell

The new arrivals to Carlisle Indian Industrial School await their transformation.

under the weight of the resources that would have to be committed to insure the integrity of the territories. For one thing, it was estimated that 50,000 troops would be needed to protect them from the ravenous hoards of settlers.

The underlying premise driving most government policy was that Native American cultures were clearly inferior to the dominant Anglo-American culture that surrounded them. Belief in this superiority reached zealous proportion with the emergence of the Theory of Manifest Destiny. Manifest Destiny was based upon the belief that America was a blessed country, a good, prosperous and just nation whose seeds must be planted across the continent. It was America's god-given and patriotic obligation to uplift all people to this advanced state. Native Americans were caught in the crosshairs as expansionist rationales found ways to justify their subjugation and destruction, and the onslaught to destroy Native American identity and exploit the rich resources of ancestral land continued unabated.

The reservation system was a geographic relocation solution; Indians west of the Mississippi were to be removed from their homeland and sent away to territories "reserved" for them. The removal was mandatory, and the United States sent troops to enforce the evacuations. The Trail of Tears tragedy was a forced relocation and movement of Native American nations from southeastern parts of the United States following the Indian Removal Act of 1830. The removal included many members of the Cherokee, Muscogee (Creek), Seminole, Chickasaw, and Choctaw nations. Forced to walk more than a thousand miles, facing hunger, disease and exhaustion, over one thousand Native Americans died.

To many, the Trail of Tears relocation was an act of ethnic cleansing of genocidal motivation, and the government's commitment to force compliance to the inequities of the reservation system brought more tragedy and death. In 1876, when the Sioux and Cheyenne defiantly left their reservations, outraged over the continual intrusion of whites into their sacred lands in the Black Hills, the government 's antagonistic response culminated in the tragic battle of Little Bighorn. In 1890, similar abusive behaviors by settlers and by the United

States government led to the Wounded Knee Massacre in South Dakota. In the years prior to the Battle of Wounded Knee, the government had continued to seize the Lakota's lands. Treaty promises to protect reservation lands from encroachment by settlers and gold miners were not honored. For one thing, the great bison herds that provided sustenance to the Lakota people were hunted to near-extinction by the settlers. As United States soldiers attempted to disarm the now desperate Lakota people, shots rang out and at least 150 men, woman and children of the Lakota were dead.

Amidst the great tragedies and great loss of life in such subjugation efforts, the government initiated other approaches. In 1869, President Grant instituted his Peace Policy to address unresolved tensions. He delegated to various Christian denominations the responsibility to educate Native Americans. Such education would transform the Native American populations and once again would be achieved by discrediting their tribal culture and traditions. Inspired missionaries went forth,

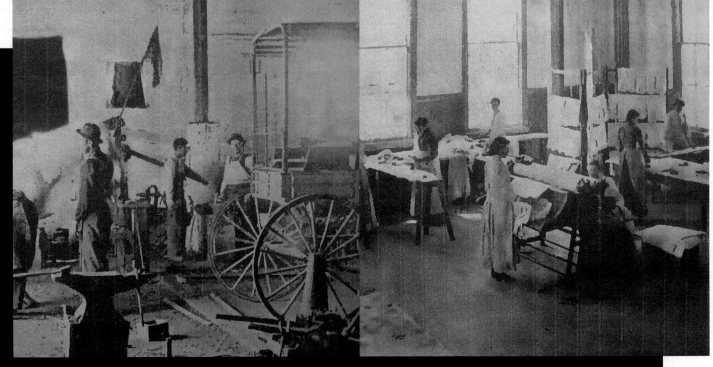

Young men at Carlisle learning the skills of the blacksmith. Young women working in the ironing room.

schools were started, and any awareness of separation of church and state was ignored. What is very rarely known is that as early as 1800 and continuing into the 1870's many tribes, including most prominently, the Cherokee, had established their own schools. Run by elders, these schools recognized the need to co-exist with the Anglo-American culture. Accordingly, education was bilingual.

# The Boarding School Experiment

Since such educational and militaristic interventions proved futile, the government in the late 19th century turned to the boarding school system. In fact, the boarding school approach was an attempt to finally get it right. Its advocates characterized earlier "solutions" as imbecilic, degrading, and cruel:

> Our policy has alternated between pauperization and extermination...and when Indians have protested against encroachment on their domain, or against being ordered from pillar to post, men ,women, and children have been ruthlessly slaughtered.

Rather than sending educators to the reservations, the government's plan now was to send Native American children to the schools. Here they would be educated in the ways of the dominant culture and mainstreamed into that culture. The belief was that such an education would provide opportunity for them to become self-supporting, productive, and industrious contributors to America.

The first step in the boarding school assimilation process was locating and removing Native American youth from their tribes. Many were taken as early as five years of age; the younger they were, the earlier the "re-education" process. Many traveled long distances; the farther they were from the contamination of their homes, the better. One of the most prominent boarding schools, the Carlisle Indian Industrial School in Pennsylvania-had students from the West and from Alaska. Seeking students, founder and superintendent Captain Richard Henry Pratt, took 62 youth from their Apache families. Many of these homesick children were stricken with tuberculosis or smallpox. Some returned home. Some stayed. Some were buried in the Carlisle graveyard.

# Assimilation and the Boarding School Education:

As most dramatically expressed by Pratt, the best way of "getting civilization into the Indian is to get the Indian into civilization." Boarding school education usually involved three components intended to promote this assimilation: religious instruction, industrial arts training, and rudimentary English language education. To ensure easeful entry into society, each student needed a practical education anchored in the vocational skills that would ensure their easeful entry into society. The curriculum of the schools offered students skills that would allow them to take on roles as trades people and domestics. Boys could choose from classes in farming, blacksmithing, carpentry, shoemaking, tailoring, and others that prepared them for real life occupations and matched their aptitudes and interests. Girls were taught baking, seamstress skills, ironing, and other domestic arts. Instruction in social etiquette and deportment was a constant feature of the education of both genders. Reading, writing, and arithmetic were mandatory components of the academic instruction. At Carlisle, enrichment opportunities for both sexes were available and included literary clubs, debate society, choir, art, and band. The band, in fact, performed at every Presidential Inaugural Parade throughout Carlisle's existence.

In many ways, the boarding school's educational philosophy mirrored the industrial education philosophy at the turn of the century. Standardized and systematic, easily replicated, instruction was intended for the masses, the pegs on the economic and mass production board. To Native American youth taught by oral traditions, personal community building, storytelling and developing practical skills in using the resources of the land, such an education was particularly foreign.

*In 2002, Assistant Secretary of the Bureau of Indian Affairs Kevin Gover called the Native American Boarding School experiment for what it was: "... a terrible act against children that brutalized them emotionally, psychologically, physically, and spiritually." The totality of its impact, he concluded, "infected, diminished, and destroyed Indian people."*

Entire Carlisle student body poses. Photos such as these were meant to show how far they had come from their "uncivilized" tribal cultures.

1899 photo of Carlisle founder Richard Henry Pratt in dress uniform, with saber. Courtesy of Cumberland County Historical Society.

## The Carlisle Indian Industrial School Experience:

To readily promote student compliance, school life at Carlisle was modeled after military life. In fact, in its earlier days, Carlisle had been a Civil War barrack, complete with guard houses, sleeping quarters, marching fields, and review stands. An ex-Civil War captain, Richard Henry Pratt was quick to create a militaristic lifestyle to match these physical features of the campus. Upon arrival, male students were given cadet style military uniforms. Girls were given Victorian style high-collared gray dresses. Boys and girls both were organized in companies, ranked, and expected to follow regimented behaviors, including regular drill practice and guard duties. Students marched to and from classes and meals. There was a guardhouse where punishment for policy violations was administered, some of it severe. Penalties for failure to behave as demanded were many and included detention in the guard house, the cleaning of the mouth with soap, and physical punishments, including "belt lines."

## "A Good Soaking"

As mentioned, boarding schools shared a predominate belief that the Native American culture was inferior. Consequently, militaristic training went beyond promoting student discipline and compliance. It was part of a larger agenda, a more pressing goal that would insure that the gains would be permanent. In the words of Pratt, the Indian must be transformed into something "nobler and higher." What that meant was they must become imitations of the white man. To do so, meant systematic regimes must be established to recast their identity and individuality. "I believe in immersing the Indians in our civilization until they are thoroughly soaked," proclaimed Pratt. The "soaking" was immediate and sustained. Upon entry, not only were youth stripped of native clothing and artifacts, but also symbolic bonfires were made of these and other belongings. Reminiscent of boot camp initiations, entrant's hair was cut. For some Native American tribal members to have their hair cut was a particularly disturbing act. For the Lakota, for example, the cutting of hair was symbolic of mourning, and there was much wailing and crying that lasted throughout the night.

Before and after photos of students in suits or formal dresses were taken to show how far they had come from their previous "sordid" existence. For five cents, supporters of the school could buy postcard photos of the youth transformed.

Pratt made sure the attack was all-inclusive. Students were forbidden to speak their native language, to socialize with members of their own tribe, to play games or sing songs that were part of their upbringing. The school goal was relentless and demeaning. As a commencement speaker proclaimed, "You cannot become truly American citizens, industrious, cultured, civilized until the Indian in you is dead." For all the rhetoric about responsible citizenship, it was not until six years after Carlisle's closing in 1918 that the Curtis Act declared all Indian people to be citizens of the United States.

# Psychological Warfare

One of the most effective components of the psychological warfare waged against children hundreds of miles away from home was the adoption of surrogate parent identity by administrators. As a way of suggesting to students his caring and mentoring while justifying his disciplinary responsibilities, Pratt frequently referred to himself as their school father. Letters written to him by students refer to him as such. Mrs. Paterson, prominent administrator of the female students, was called their mother. As an additional way to be an invasive presence in the children's lives, Pratt often placed himself on the grandstand during ceremonies and at overseer positions throughout campus.

This ubiquitous "Man-in-the- Stand" identity was explicitly acknowledged in the two school publications, *the Indian Helper and the Redman*. Although written by students, all material was edited by staff referring to themselves as Man-in-the- Stand figures. Various administrative figures represented this persona, all providing an insinuating voice that approved and directed the publications' content. Occasionally, they penned editorials with Man-in-the Stand bylines.

## The Outing System

To assure no regression to their "savage" ways, the Outing System was created. Indian children did not return home during the summer months but instead were placed with families in the community. They became a source of cheap labor at the home and on the farm. In some cases, children stayed with families throughout the winter as well and attended local public schools.

Upon graduation, students were told to "go on the hunt" in the East, find worthwhile jobs and become productive citizens. The perils and shame of going home were made clear in a commencement excerpt: "...not one in ten will find anything at home worth going home for.

Depiction of young women and men lining up to enter cafeteria at Carlisle.

At most of their homes there is idleness which kills. Dirt and filth and evil practices and rot...."

The unfortunate reality was that of the 12,000 Indian children who attended Carlisle during its 39 year existence, most returned to the reservation. Only 158 students graduated from Carlisle. The outing system was a failure. When they returned home, many felt lost, unable to fully participate in tribal life after having been exposed to the boarding school experience. Sadly, the "soaking" made them unable to live within either society.

## An Admission of Wrongdoing

Unfortunately, the boarding school system was often inhumane and degrading, and generally ineffective. Assistant Secretary of the Bureau of Indian Affairs Kevin Gover in 2002 called the Native American Boarding School experiment for what it was: "... a terrible act against children that brutalized them emotionally, psychologically, physically, and spiritually." The totality of its impact, he concluded, "infected, diminished, and destroyed Indian people." Over 125,000 Native American youth spread across the country in twenty-five schools experienced this nightmare before it ended.

# Baseball Marches onto the Field

By the late 19th century, baseball was well on it ways towards become part of the fabric of American life. Promoted as the national pastime, it was portrayed as a game for everyone, including the masses. From street urchin to banker's son, all were offered a chance to compete fairly and fiercely. The patriotic and egalitarian essence of the game was reaffirmed in the opening remarks of Baseball Commissioner Kenesaw Mountain Landis during the 1939 centennial which celebrated the opening of the Hall of Fame in Cooperstown, New York:

> Baseball- America's National Game- is one hundred years old this year...It has marched side by side with the development of this great nation...baseball is the personification of Americanism- American sportsmanship, team-play, aggressiveness. This year Uncle Sam is giving a gigantic birthday party to baseball. It's Everybody's game, Everybody's party.

Sixty years earlier, Theodore Roosevelt had declared baseball to be a "most admirable and characteristic American game." As early as the late nineteenth century, magazines, sports journals, newspapers, league publications, etc., trumpeted the qualities of the mind and spirit that the game was said to foster. Victory on and off the field was said to be brought about by decisiveness, quick thinking, physical conditioning, clean living, cooperation, and self-reliance. Youth companion magazines featured young baseball-playing role model protagonists such as Frank Merriwell, Fred Fearnot and Jack Standfast who displayed their namesake traits as they battled forces of greed, laziness and deception.

Baseball soon became part of a social gospel intended to promote the physical and mental health of the working class. This gospel met with resistance from the establishment, many of which objected to the use of public recreation areas to play ball on Sunday not only because it violated Sabbath rules but also because it invited the migration of undesirable street urchins eager to escape for a day the grinding world of industrial America.

A tribute to its success in promoting itself as a morally and physically invigorating activity, baseball was incorporated into prison rehabilitation programs.

By 1914, both San Quentin and Sing Sing had teams and the Atlanta Penitentiary was part of an eight club league. And if the game was seen as promoting the distinctive character traits that would build character and preparedness for reintroduction into society, it also provided a unique opportunity for inmates to play and beat outside visiting teams, teams made up of respected societal figures- insurance agents, electrical workers, stock exchange financiers, etc..

Advertisement connecting the virtues of baseball and American manhood.

Weekly youth magazines often used baseball-playing protagonists such as Fred Fearnot to inspire young boys to become models of character and decisive action.

No doubt Carlisle and other boarding schools saw the use of baseball as a way to further erase Native American identity while offering a way to develop mainstream American virtues. Baseball and other sports were part of the assimilation strategy. Composed of the disenfranchised and isolated, boarding school teams such as Carlisle often played top level competition from surrounding towns and collegiate teams. Native Americans thus were given a rare opportunity to show their worth, to take on the establishment in fair and strong competition.

As much as it allowed Native Americans to show their considerable talents, baseball at all levels, from professional leagues, to local teams, to barnstorming teams such as the Nebraska Indians, intentionally perpetuated the stereotypic behaviors associated with Native Americans. To do so, made turnstiles spin and newspaper bins empty. In journalistic reports, Indians were described as stoical beings, as savages, as bloodthirsty warriors. They were said to possess the keen eyes of the hunter or the mesmerizing presence of the shaman. Victories were called "scalpings" and teams were "on the warpath." Created tribal names were given to the players. "Chief" was a frequent title. Traveling teams were quick to create entertainment techniques popular in the Wild West show traditions.

Degrading depictions of Bender as a wily savage :
(Top)- Searching for fallen wallets on the train.
(Bottom)- Casting a hypnotic spell on the opposition.

Bender preparing to pitch a World Series game for Mr. Connie Mack's Philadelphia A's.

Traveling baseball teams' promotions exploited common images associated with the Native Americans.

# 2-GAMES DAILY-2
## Afternoon 3 P.M.

## A Superior Attraction
### WORTH GOING MILES TO SEE.

### This Team scored shutouts in 14 different States last season

A 13-inning game was played here yesterday between Foster Stevens and Cherokee Indians. Score 1-0, favor of Indians. From the first ball pitched until the winning run crossed the plate, it was a great game of ball and enjoyed by about 1,000 fans, crowd being kept down by threatening weather. The Red Men lived up to all the nice things said of them in advance notices and demonstrated themselves to be one of the

# DON'T FAIL TO WITNESS
## THE
# GREATEST GAME
## Of the Season

# LINE-UP OF INDIANS

| Indian | Translation | Position |
|---|---|---|
| PENOBSQUIS | SPOTTED TAIL | 1st Base |
| GUISPANSIS | WHITE CLOUD | Pitcher |
| APOHAQUI | THREE RIVERS | Left Field |
| WAUMBEEKA | SCAR FACE | 2d Base |
| SECONTEE | RED HORSE | 3d Base |
| ITASCA | SITTING BULL, Jr. | Center Field |
| NATALONITA | MAN-AFRAID-OF-HIMSELF | Short Stop |
| SASQUIN | BIG BEAVER | Right Field |
| AGUDWUM | NAVAJO | Catcher |
| COBOSSEE | SWIFT HORSE | Substitute |
| MINNETONKA | BAD MAN CHARLIE | Pitcher |
| OBASCO | BLACK EAGLE | Pitcher |

If its reports are to be believed, this team enjoyed great success and traveled afar, including Chicago, Grand Rapids, and San Francisco. Whether the translations of the player's names are to be believed is another story.

EXCHANGE WAR CLUB for Ball Bat

*Indian Athletes Who Have Invaded Big Leagues of the Paleface Are Today Among the Most Brilliant Players in the Great American Game*

Early baseball card of Jim Thorpe

Four Native American stars of the Great American Game, all of whom had to endure demeaning depictions such as those in the headline.

Boarding schools, especially Carlisle, used their sports programs to draw local and national attention and reaffirm their success in reforming the Indian. Nevertheless, money and propaganda aside, baseball offered a rare opportunity to stand straight on a normally crooked field. Among other things, it provided an opportunity to reconfigure the warrior tradition. Years later, many boarding school students spoke with pride of victories earned, of a sense of community and a feeling of dignity provided by sports, including baseball.

Perhaps baseball also allowed them to address their abiding sense of grievance. No doubt there is a proud payback defiance in New York Giant catcher John Meyer's remark that Native American success in baseball proved that Indians could excel in "the white man's principal sport." Jim Thorpe confronted a manager who called him "a dumb Indian." Mose Yellow Horse did not allow Ty Cobb's racial slurs to go uncontested.

In all, one hundred and twenty six Native Americans made it to the big leagues. On town fields, on city streets, in amateur and semi-professional teams, thousands of others competed. The irony was that the game intended to be an instrument of cultural conversion was an empowering way for Native Americans to keep their pride, to show what they could do. For the moment at least, it was "Everybody's game, Everybody's party."

Early baseball card of "Chief" Meyers

Philadelphia A's Manager Connie Mack (center, derby hat) seated. Charles Bender standing, second from right, last row). A mentor of sorts to Bender, Mack called him the one pitcher he would want on the mound when the game was on the line.

1903 Carlisle Indian School baseball team. The coach shown is Glenn "Pop" Warner of football renown. Courtesy of Cumberland County Historical Society

Bender as a student at Carlisle, 1902. Courtesy of Cumberland County Historical Society

Connie Mack seems to be celebrating Bender in this photo of the 1911 World Champion Philadelphia Athletics plate. Bender's best year for Connie came in 1910 with a remarkable 23-5 record and 1.58 ERA.

# About the Author

In the middle of the wonderfully hot summer day,

In the beginning of our day,

We played ball in our white tee shirts and canvas sneakers.

Our moms called; our dads smiled.

Rainbow belted dreams glittering with dust and sweat.

Now, rounding third base,

I pray that we all found a way to stand.

An English teacher and curriculum development specialist for over thirty years, Greg Rubano currently develops anti-bullying and intolerance programs. He has just completed another baseball themed book for youth: *Before the Babe, the Emperor: Napoleon Lajoie*

# This book is a donation from

# The Independent Order of Odd Fellows

**Building a Better World through Friendship.Love,and Truth**